IMAGES
of Aviation

PAN AM

IMAGES
of Aviation

PAN AM

Lynn M. Homan and Thomas Reilly

ARCADIA
PUBLISHING

Published by Arcadia Publishing
Charleston SC, Chicago IL, Portsmouth NH, San Francisco CA

Printed in the United States of America

Library of Congress Catalog Card Number: 99-069393

For all general information contact Arcadia Publishing at:
Telephone 843-853-2070
Fax 843-853-0044
E-mail sales@arcadiapublishing.com
For customer service and orders:
Toll-Free 1-888-313-2665

Visit us on the Internet at www.arcadiapublishing.com

CONTENTS

INTRODUCTION

The story of Pan American World Airways is as much the story of Juan T. Trippe as it is an account of airplanes, airports, passengers, pilots, flight attendants, and glamorous destinations. From the very beginning, it was unarguably his airline, molded through his machinations, vision, motivation, and politics. As the company moved throughout the world building airfields from jungles, crossing oceans, and forcing the development of new airplanes, it was his airline, his vision. As management and corporate board members were added, things did not change; the company continued to be Trippe's. He decided what was going to be done and so it was. When Pan American World Airways ceased flying in 1991 after 64 years of service, and years after Juan Trippe was long dead, it was still his airline. More than any other airline pioneer, Juan Trippe, for better or for worse, made Pan Am what it was.

In 1927, several airlines—Atlantic, Gulf and Caribbean Airways; Pan American Airways; and Aviation Corporation of America—were founded. The three companies each wanted to begin air service in Latin America. Atlantic, Gulf and Caribbean Airways, formed by Richard F. Hoyt and Reed Chambers, had a corporate structure and money but no equipment. In July, Pan American Airways, headed by John K. Montgomery, Richard D. Bevier, and George Grant Mason, had received a mail contract from the United States government to be inaugurated by October 1927, over the Key West, Florida-to-Havana, Cuba route. Cuban President Gerardo Machado had granted exclusive landing rights in Cuba to Juan Trippe, John Hambleton, and Cornelius Whitney of the Aviation Corporation of America.

When the United States Postal Service became involved, Assistant Postmaster General W. Irving Glover strongly suggested a merger of the three entities. Officials of the three airlines agreed to merge the companies under the new name of Aviation Corporation of the Americas. Juan Trippe, at only 28 years of age, became president and general manager of Pan American, the company's operating subsidiary.

Regular airmail service began from Key West to Havana on October 28, 1927. The first flight in a Fokker F-VII, named the *General Machado*, carried 772 pounds of mail. Pilot Hugh Wells, navigator Edwin C. Musick, and John Johansen, engineer-mechanic, made the flight in 1 hour and 20 minutes. Thousands of insistent people had inundated Captain J.E. Whitbeck, Pan Am's Key West representative, for the opportunity to fly on the first regularly scheduled flight to Havana. It did not matter that the flight was going to carry only mail; they still wanted to fly.

Over 700 people witnessed the departure of the *General Machado* from Key West's Meacham Airport. The eight-passenger Fokker F-VII cost $45,000 and had been built especially for Pan American for the Key West-to-Havana service. Scheduled for 8 a.m., the departure was delayed until 8:25 a.m. because Wells had not arrived in Key West until early that morning. A photographer for the *International News* was on hand to record the day's events for posterity. After Cuba received nearly a foot of rain in a 24-hour period, turning Havana's Camp Columbia, the government aviation field, into a sea of mud, the return flight to Key West was postponed until the next morning. An aviation legend had begun.

From its relatively obscure inauguration as a mail carrier on a 90-mile mail run from Florida to Cuba, Pan Am's route system grew to span the globe. Juan Trippe wanted his company to be more than just an airline, however far-reaching. When it came to transportation or aerospace, his objective was for Pan Am to be everything to everyone, capable of influencing the lives of people and the politics of nations. The company that would eventually become famous for its blue-and-white-world logo grew into a conglomerate of hotels, airlines, business jets, real estate, a helicopter service, and even a guided missiles range division.

The Intercontinental Hotel Corporation grew from a single-hotel operation in South America to nearly 100 first-class hotels around the world. Eventually Forum Hotels, a lower-priced chain, was also added. The Business Jets Division, headquartered at Teterboro Airport, New Jersey, offered a twin-engine business jet. The Fan Jet Falcon was sold to hundreds of customers, including royalty, Hollywood celebrities, airlines, and the chief executive officers of major American and European companies. New York Airways offered passengers scheduled helicopter service between New York City's Pan Am Building and John F. Kennedy International Airport. The Guided Missiles Range Division served many functions as a contractor to the U.S. Air Force at Cape Kennedy Missile Test Center, the Eastern Test Range, the Space Nuclear Propulsion Facility at Jackson Flats, Nevada, and the Churchill Research Range, Fort Churchill, Canada. The company also supported other government and military projects such as the U.S. Navy's Trident program and various National Aeronautics and Space Administration missions. Eventually, Pan Am's subsidiaries would prove to be more profitable than Juan Trippe's core business, his airline operation.

Pan American could be considered a corporate Cinderella—a rags-to-riches-and-back-again phenomenon. During wartime, Pan Am played a leadership role. In the aviation industry, the airline's achievements were legendary. However, like most successful enterprises, it had its share of flaws and failures, tragedies, and disasters.

Pan Am was long known as the "world's most experienced airline" and the company that made the "going great." During its last years, Pan Am was described as "troubled" and "financially ailing." After Juan Trippe retired as chairman and chief executive officer in 1968, instability at the top quickly followed. One president after another was unable to restore Pan American to its once exalted status. Massive financial losses, the sale of valuable assets, and a constantly shrinking route system characterized the final decade of the airline's life.

Pan American should be recognized and remembered for what it truly was—a global pioneer, a conqueror of oceans, and the stimulus behind new technology. Its firsts are numerous. Pan Am was the first airline to use radio communications (1928), to employ cabin attendants and to serve meals aloft (1929), to operate scheduled transpacific service (1939), and to complete an around-the-world flight (1942). It was also the first to order American-manufactured commercial jet aircraft (1955), to operate scheduled transatlantic service with American-built jets (1958), to order the Boeing 747 (1966), and to offer around-the-world service with the Boeing 747 (1971).

From its origin in Key West, Florida, to the entire world as its eventual destination, this is the story of Pan Am.

One

BIRTH OF AN AIRLINE

Pan American's first mail contract, FAM 4, was issued on July 19, 1927, and granted the airline the authority to operate between Key West, Florida, and Havana, Cuba. Two Fokker F-VII trimotors had been ordered but not yet received. The new company was required to begin airmail service by October 19th or risk losing the operating rights to Cuba. Construction of the company-commissioned runway at Key West was not yet finished. Pan Am's president, Juan Trippe, had big problems. In order to comply with the requirements of FAM 4, Pan American Airways chartered a Fairchild FC-2 float plane named *La Niña* from West Indian Aerial Express for Pan Am's inaugural flight from Key West to Havana. Charter pilot Cy Caldwell departed Key West at 8:30 a.m. on October 19th with seven sacks of mail containing 30,000 letters. Caldwell charged Pan Am $175 for the 1-hour-and-20-minute first flight from Key West to Havana. Juan Trippe's Pan Am was now in business. (Private Collection.)

Few good things emerged from Russia's harsh Bolshevik Revolution. Igor I. Sikorsky was one. The revolution led to the immigration of Russia's preeminent aerospace engineer to America where his contributions to the infant field of aviation proved of inestimable value. In 1927, Igor Sikorsky became linked with Juan Trippe, president of the newly formed Pan American Airlines. (Private Collection.)

On December 7, 1927, Pan American took delivery of its first Sikorsky aircraft, a Sikorsky S-36 amphibian. Trippe wanted the S-36 for survey flights into South America and the Caribbean. While the S-36 was not perfect, it proved to Trippe that an amphibian was the right aircraft for his airline, at least until airports could be built. (Private Collection.)

On October 31, 1928, Pan American introduced the eight-passenger Sikorsky S-38 into service. Known as the "ugly ducking," "flying tadpole," and "a collection of airplane parts flying in formation," the S-38 was described as a "shoetree onto which a wing, tail booms, and engines had been attached." While the S-38 might have been ugly, it was unarguably the aircraft that was largely responsible for the early successes of Pan American. (Florida State Archives.)

From left to right André Priester, chief engineer; Juan Trippe; and James Eaton, general traffic manager, pose in front of a Sikorsky S-38. The S-38 was the right aircraft for the time. Without the S-38, it is extremely doubtful that Pan American could have pulled off one of its earliest coups—the conquest and monopoly of Latin American air routes. (Florida State Archives.)

On July 13, 1928, Pan Am was awarded FAM 5, an airmail route from Miami to Cristobal, Panama, via Cuba and the Yucatan. The once-a-week round trip would pay $2 per mile and was scheduled to begin February 4, 1929. When Charles Lindbergh went to work for Trippe in early 1929 as a technical advisor, his first assignment was to fly the inaugural trip to Panama. Nine days and 4,000 miles later, Lindbergh (center, dressed in dark suit and helmet) returned to Miami. (Florida State Archives.)

Within two years of its inaugural flight, Pan Am's air network covered 12,000 miles and served 23 countries in the Caribbean and Central and South America. With the implicit support of the United States government, Pan Am was providing a transportation system that allowed the United States to control economic expansion throughout Latin America. Pan Am claimed to have the "largest air service in the world." (Private Collection.)

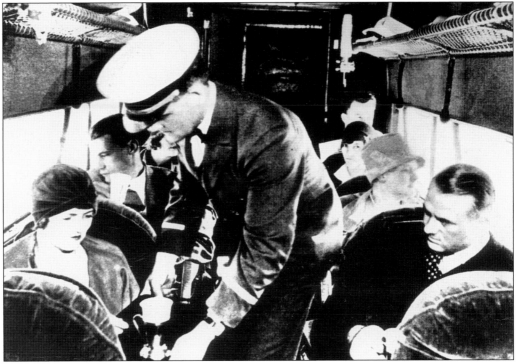

Beverage service was provided onboard a Pan Am trimotor Fokker F-VII. In 1929, Pan American became the first airline to employ cabin attendants and serve meals aloft. The eight-seat Fokker, manufactured in New Jersey, boasted a passenger amenity that few airplanes of the era offered— a toilet. (Private Collection.)

Pan American's passenger service from Key West to Havana did not begin until January 16, 1928. The service was immediately popular. For a one-way fare of $50, more than 1,100 tickets were sold the first year. The airline's operation was sophisticated by comparison. Pan Am's three Fokker F-VIIs, each costing $45,000, were outfitted with airborne radio equipment. (Private Collection.)

Little more than a small air taxi service, Compañia Mexicana de Aviación started in August 1924. Although the four founders, George L. Rihl, C.V. Schlaet, Archie Piper, and W.L. Mallory, were Americans, the company was regarded as a Mexican company. Mexicana's route structure was sparse and utilitarian; the company made its money through short hops throughout Mexico. Cargoes carried usually included gold for oil field payrolls. (Private Collection.)

Trippe's personal dream of manifest destiny continued when he purchased Compañia Mexicana de Aviación in January 1929. Trippe wanted operating rights to fly within Mexico. With the purchase of Mexicana, he had them. Shortly after the acquisition of Compañia Mexicana de Aviación, Trippe was awarded Foreign Airmail route number 8; the company could now carry mail and passengers from Brownsville, Texas, to points in Mexico and on to the Canal Zone. (Private Collection.)

Pan Am's original United States terminus, Key West, proved to be impractical for a passenger service operation. Pan Am abandoned Key West and moved its base of operations to Miami in October 1928. Several hangars were constructed, and plans were soon in the works for a grand new terminal. Having the airline headquartered in Miami made it much more convenient to connect with passengers arriving from the northeast by train. (Florida State Archives.)

West Indian Aerial Express provided service over an 800-mile route from Haiti to Puerto Rico. When the foreign airmail contract was offered, both Trippe and West Indian's owner submitted bids for the mail route. FAM 6 was awarded to Pan Am on July 14, 1928, even though West Indian had flown the advertised route previously. Without the mail subsidy, West Indian could not compete; Trippe acquired the company. (Private Collection.)

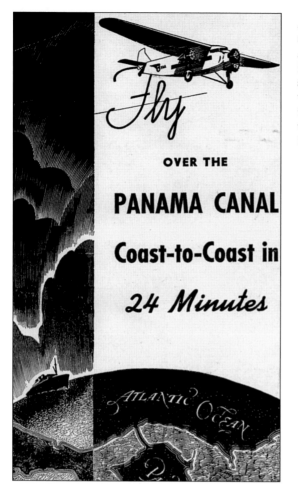

An early Pan Am brochure advertised a flight in a Fokker trimotor from the Atlantic Ocean to the Pacific Ocean in only 24 minutes. This was possible since the coast-to-coast width of Panama varies from 30 to 120 miles. By following the Panama Canal, Pan Am's route was approximately 50 miles in length. (Private Collection.)

Pan American's first timetable, dated January 1928, featured a one-way fare of $50 from Key West to Havana and extolled the virtues of a flight aboard an eight-passenger Fokker as compared to the long trip by steamer. The brochure asked, "How many times have you stood on the deck of a steamer, tossing in a rough sea and enviously watched the gulls wheeling and dipping 'round the vessel?'" (Private Collection.)

Pan American's "Plane Train" advertising promised speed, comfort, a bargain, and exotic destinations. From the dreariness and cold of winter, Americans could now escape in a matter of hours instead of days to the warmth of tropical island paradises such as Havana or Nassau. In many early advertisements such as this one, the name of the legendary Charles Lindbergh was used to promote Pan American. (Private Collection.)

Juan Trippe made good use of his government connections in Washington as he added new routes for his airline. Between May 29, 1928, and March 2, 1929, Pan Am was awarded Foreign Airmail routes 4, 5, 6, 7, 8, and 9, allowing service to Havana, Nassau, Santiago, Port Au Prince, Santo Domingo, and San Juan. Each route provided Pan American $2 per mile in mail revenue. (Private Collection.)

In 1917, Juan Trippe, like many young men his age, left college and joined the Marines. A transfer to the Navy allowed him to do what he wanted to do—fly airplanes. Following ground school at Massachusetts Institute of Technology, he soloed above Long Island Sound in a Curtiss Jenny. At Hampton Roads, Virginia, he received instruction in flying boats. Commissioned as an ensign in the United States Naval Air Reserve, Trippe's next duty station was Pensacola Naval Air Station. At Pensacola he became a radio instructor and acquired proficiency in flying night bombing missions. Trippe finally got his wish and was en route to combat in Europe when the war ended. Trippe returned to the United States and Yale University in February 1919. Following graduation, he apprenticed at the Wall Street firm of Lee, Higginson, & Company. There, as at Yale, he developed friendships with the sons of some of America's wealthiest families. When Trippe entered the airline business in 1923, he frequently called on these friendships. (Florida State Archives.)

Two

THE EARLY YEARS

A Pan American baggage tag from 1929 featured one of the airline's planes flying above a tropical scene. By 1930, Pan Am operated over a route system of 19,190 miles and flew 100,000 miles each week. Route development was rapid, as evidenced by this early baggage tag that showed flights from Miami to Cuba, Haiti, Santo Domingo, Puerto Rico, Nicaragua, Panama, Costa Rica, Honduras, Mexico, Guatemala, Salvador, and British Honduras. From the early days of the first flight from Key West to Havana in 1927, Pan Am had grown by quantum leaps. Trippe's company now boasted a fleet of over 100 land and sea airplanes and 1,600 employees. Much of the rapid growth came about as a result of acquisition of other airlines. Between 1928 and 1932, Trippe would acquire ten Latin American airlines, giving his company operating rights and thousands of miles of routes throughout Central and South America. (Private Collection.)

Charles Lindbergh was pictured at the controls of a Pan American Airways' Sikorsky S-38 amphibian at Miami on February 4, 1929. As technical advisor for Pan American, Lindbergh was assigned the job of opening up FAM 5 from Miami to Panama. Fifty thousand people showed up on the morning of February 4th to see Lindbergh take off. Three days later, Lindbergh was in Cristobal. The mail had been delivered, and FAM 5 was in force. (Florida State Archives.)

Anne Morrow Lindbergh, Betty Trippe, Charles Lindbergh, and Juan Trippe arrived at Dinner Key in Miami, Florida, in September 1929, following their extended 7,000-mile South American survey flight. The trip had hardly been a vacation. Accompanied by a copilot and radio operator, from dawn to dusk, the travelers flew from one country to another, meeting with heads of state, business leaders, and thousands of well-wishers. Juan Trippe met with the heads of 16 governments in only 20 days. (Florida State Archives.)

Juan Trippe and Pan American did everything possible to capitalize on the good name of Charles Lindbergh and his association with the company. "Flying the Lindbergh Trail," an early piece of Pan American advertising, was an obvious attempt to trade on the reputation of Charles Lindbergh, unarguably commercial aviation's most well-known ambassador of good will. Serving as a technical advisor to Pan Am, Lindbergh contracted with Trippe for a four-year period during which he was paid $10,000 per year. In January 1928, Lindbergh conducted an aerial tour of 14 Latin American countries and the Canal Zone. Following this 9,000-mile trip, the route that Lindbergh followed was christened the Lindbergh Circle. Trippe was quick to capitalize on such a newsworthy event with Pan American's "Lindbergh Trail" throughout a dozen Latin American countries. (Private Collection.)

Pan American promised passengers an air cruise throughout the West Indies, the Bahamas, and Mexico. The hyperbole of a copywriter promised "Cocktail time in Havana," "mysterious Haiti," and "the land of Columbus." The cost of the 20-day, all-luxury air cruise was $890. Those coming from the northeast traveled by train to Miami. From that point, the flight itinerary included stops in Cuba, Haiti, Santo Domingo, and Puerto Rico. (Private Collection.)

This image was just one section of a four-frame stylized aerial route map from Miami to Havana, the West Indies, and the Bahamas. A mixed fleet of Pan Am aircraft, including Fokkers and Sikorskys, were flying hundreds of weekly flights that originated in Miami and ended in exotic locations in the Caribbean. (Private Collection.)

Early airmail labels were used for Pan Am's Caribbean routes. Pan American promised that mail that traveled over its several foreign airmail routes "will save weeks in exchange of correspondence." Featured on this label was one of the three Sikorsky S-40s that Pan American placed into service in November 1931. Reliability of the Sikorsky S-40 was unsurpassed. Thousands of flights were made with a nearly perfect on-time record. (Private Collection.)

This Pan American Airways' eight-passenger Fokker F-VII was named the *General Machado* in honor of the Cuban dictator Gerardo Machado. Powered by three Wright J-4 engines, the Fokker was capable of flying the Florida-to-Cuba route in 1 hour and 20 minutes. The fuselage was constructed of welded steel tubing and was covered with fabric or plywood skins. (Florida State Archives.)

WINGS

For the GREAT TRADE ROUTE

NYRBA

AIR LINES

EXPORT TRADE EXTENSION DEPARTMENT
NYRBA AIR LINES
NEW YORK RIO AND BUENOS AIRES LINE INC.
420 LEXINGTON AVENUE NEW YORK CITY

In 1930, New York, Rio, and Buenos Aires line (NYRBA) operated a route system from Miami southward down the east coast of South America to Buenos Aires, Argentina. The company had been started by Ralph A. O'Neill and incorporated on April 29, 1929. NYRBA's first service began four months later and operated over a route between Buenos Aires, Argentina, and Montevideo, Uruguay, with service over the Andes into Santiago. (Private Collection.)

By the end of 1929, Ralph O'Neill's NYRBA had a fleet of four Sikorsky S-38s, one Consolidated Commodore, and three Ford trimotors, one of which is pictured in this photograph. O'Neill, the company's president, appeared, at least on paper, to have the perfect credentials to operate an airline. A highly decorated World War I aviator, he was quite experienced in the aviation business, including tenure as a salesman with Boeing Airplane Company. (Florida State Archives.)

New York, Rio, and Buenos Aires line seemed to have all of the ingredients for success. The company's financial backing was unparalleled in the airline industry. Well-known backers included Reuben Fleet, the president of Consolidated Aircraft Company, and James H. Rand Jr., president of Remington Rand Company. The company had easily been able to raise $6 million. From the start, however, NYRBA lost hundreds of thousands of dollars each month. (Private Collection.)

On August 19, 1930, Pan American purchased the assets of NYRBA for $2 million. Along with the South American routes came 32 aircraft, including 14 Consolidated Commodore flying boats. When Trippe asked O'Neill to work for him, a livid O'Neill responded, "You can steal my house, but you can't ask me to run it for you." Purchase of NYRBA gave Pan Am a virtual monopoly on South American routes. (Florida State Archives.)

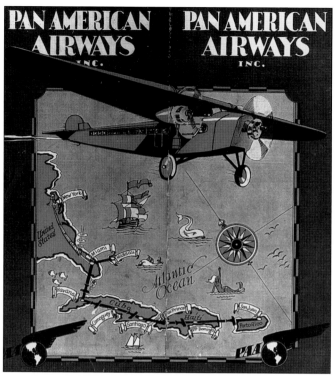

By 1930, Pan American Airways operated over a route system of 19,190 miles and flew 100,000 miles each week. Route development was rapid, as evidenced by this early advertisement, with flights from Miami to Nassau, Havana, Camaguey, Santiago, Port au Prince, Santo Domingo, and San Juan. No longer operating out of Key West, Pan Am had moved its base of operations to Miami in October 1928. (Private Collection.)

In 1928, Pan American acquired New York Airways, Inc. The company, with an operating route in the northeast United States from New York to Atlantic City to Baltimore to Washington, was relatively meaningless to Trippe's international airline. When Walter F. Brown, postmaster general of the United States, suggested ". . . the abandonment by the Pan American Co. of the domestic field in the United States," Trippe sold New York Airways to Eastern Air Transport in July 1931. (Private Collection.)

Juan Trippe's objective was to encompass and control the Caribbean, Central America, and South America. While encircling the Caribbean, Pan Am began active acquisition, primarily for operating rights of other companies. When Pan Am wanted to operate in Columbia, Sociedad Colombo-Alemana de Transportes Aéreos (SCADTA) was secretly acquired. Founded in 1919 by Peter Paul von Bauer, an Austrian, SCADTA was a great concern for the United States government. (Private Collection.)

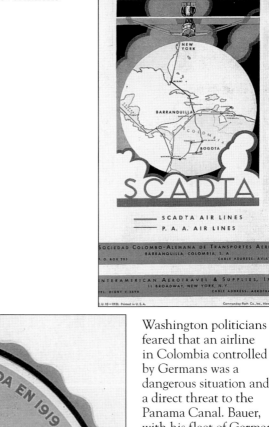

Washington politicians feared that an airline in Colombia controlled by Germans was a dangerous situation and a direct threat to the Panama Canal. Bauer, with his fleet of German manufactured aircraft, was denied subsidized United States foreign airmail contracts. Because of financial difficulties, Bauer sold 84.4 percent of SCADTA's stock to the Aviation Corporation of the Americas. Trippe now had a through route to the west coast of South America. (Private Collection.)

Pan American promised the "Shortest Time to Sunshine" in this advertisement from 1930. The airline was now offering service to 32 Latin American countries. Much of this rapid development and growth had come about because of the assistance of Charles Lindbergh. Uncharacteristically, Trippe gave much of the credit to Lindbergh for the successful expansion. He stated, "Lindbergh was the genius. I don't mean Lindbergh's great flying career, but his ability to look ahead to develop air transport in a way to bring the world closer together." To this point, Pan Am's list of firsts was impressive. By 1930, Pan Am was the first American airline to operate a permanent international air service, to operate land planes over water on regularly scheduled flights, to operate multi-engine aircraft permanently in scheduled transportation, to carry emergency lifesaving equipment, to use multiple flight crews, and to develop an airport and airways traffic control system. In truth, it had taken thousands of people to develop the airline to this point. Pilots, mechanics, and technicians were all as important to the growth as either Trippe or Lindbergh. (Private Collection.)

As the Pan American route system grew, the need for aircraft with a longer range and greater passenger-carrying ability resulted. Once again, Pan American turned to Igor Sikorsky. The new Sikorsky S-40 provided the necessary payload and range. Designed in part by Charles Lindbergh, Juan Trippe, and his engineers, the S-40 became the first aircraft to be configured to an airline's specifications. (Florida State Archives.)

Juan Trippe placed orders for three Sikorsky S-40 flying boats on December 20, 1929. Powered by four Pratt and Whitney 575-horsepower direct-drive Hornet engines, the S-40 was capable of carrying 24 passengers a distance of approximately 950 miles. With a full load of 40 passengers, the S-40's range was reduced to only 500 miles. (Private Collection.)

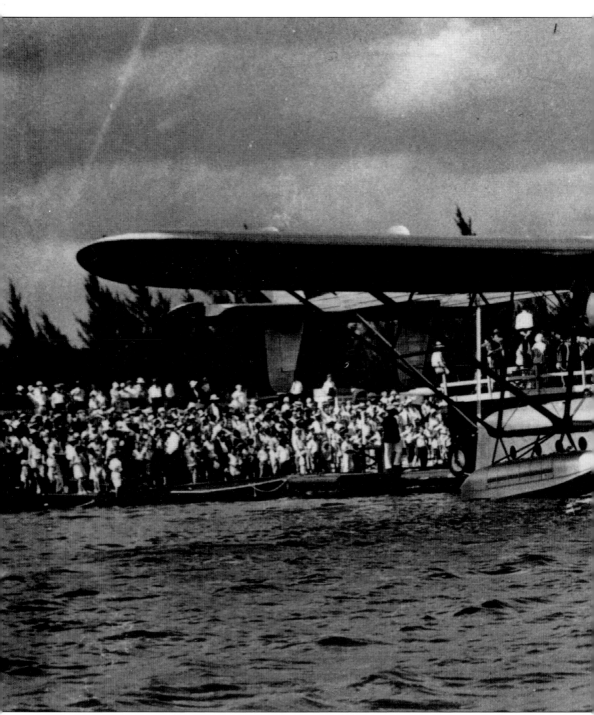

Featuring the trademark Sikorsky twin tail booms, an S-40 seaplane was moored at the anchored barge off Dinner Key, Biscayne Bay, Miami. Charles Lindbergh called the S-40 the "flying forest" because of a proliferation of gangly wing struts. The cockpit was designed to greatly reduce or eliminate the effects of water spray on takeoffs and landings. Pan American's first Sikorsky S-40 entered service on November 19, 1931, as Charles Lindbergh took off from Miami for a flight to

the Canal Zone. The reliability of the S-40 was unsurpassed. Thousands of flights were made over Pan American's route system with a nearly perfect on-time arrival rate. With a purchase price of $125,000 each, the Sikorsky S-40 was little more than a larger, more aerodynamic S-38 with four engines. Only three S-40s were built. (Florida State Archives.)

Passengers prepare to board a Sikorsky S-40 at Dinner Key. This was the first aircraft in Pan Am's fleet to be christened "clipper," establishing a long-standing tradition of all Pan Am aircraft being called clippers. On October 12, 1931, Mrs. Herbert Hoover, wife of the president of the United States, smashed a bottle of Caribbean water against the hull of a Sikorsky flying boat, christening it *Clipper America*. (Florida State Archives.)

A Pan American Sikorsky S-40 flying boat prepares to land at Dinner Key in 1932. Aboard the Pan American clippers, all was as nautical as possible. The pilot was called captain; the copilot was the first officer. Speed was reckoned as knots and time according to bells. The S-40 featured such passenger service amenities as a well-equipped galley, electric range, refrigerator, and separate lavatories for men and women. (Florida State Archives.)

Juan Trippe frequently saw threats where none existed. Such was the case with Compañia Nacional Cubana de Aviación Curtiss S.A. Although the company was little more than an air taxi operating over an 800-mile route, Trippe nonetheless wanted the airline. The small Cuban airline was acquired by Pan Am in May 1932. The airline's name was changed to Cia. Nacional Cubana de Aviación. (Private Collection.)

Santiago - Antilla - Cayo Mambí - Baracoa - Guantánamo - Isla de Pinos
AS - CENTRO Y SUR AMERICA

Cía. Nacional Cubana de Aviación
División de la Pan American Airways
NEPTUNO No. 2 - TELEFS. A-2222 y A-6664

In 1932, Pan American Airways System operated over 22,000 miles of airways and served 32 countries. According to this August 1932 timetable, the one-way fare from Miami to Buenos Aires, Argentina, was $666. A 10 percent discount was offered for round-trip tickets. As did many other pieces of Pan Am advertising, the timetable featured the four-engine Sikorsky S-40. (Private Collection.)

PAN AMERICAN AIR WAYS
JULY 1932

PUBLIC RELATIONS
FILE COPY

Kenneth W. Thompson

"ROLLING DOWN TO RIO"

NEW CONNECTING SCHEDULES SPEED AIR MAIL TO 25 COUNTRIES
TWO PAN AMERICAN EXPEDITIONS TO STUDY NORTHERN TRANSATLANTIC

NEW YORK SETS AIR EXPRESS RECORD   NEW FLIGHT PERSONNEL INSIGNIA
CLIPPERS ON TRANSCARIBBEAN   MOTOR SYCHRONIZER DEVELOPED

What's Going On . . .
CARIBBEAN · WESTERN · BRAZILIAN DIVISIONS · PAN AMERICAN GRACE

In 1932, *Pan American Air Ways* magazine advertised, "New connecting schedules speed airmail to 25 countries." The first five years of Pan American's history had been characterized by incredible accomplishment. It had not been easy. Pan Am lost $1,000 in its first three months of operation in 1927. Between 1928 and 1930, the company lost $300,000. Not until 1931 did Pan Am become profitable, earning $100,000, followed by earnings of $700,000 in 1932. Trippe preached safety first, excellent customer service, and consistency in his airline operation. Service received in Havana, Rio de Janeiro, or San Juan was expected to be as good as that in Miami. The company employed weather forecasters and used radio and weather stations throughout its system. The airline built landing fields and airports, sometimes out of jungles. Pan Am's service record was impressive. The United States Post Office rated Pan Am at 99 percent, in recognition of the airline's reliability. With success, however, there was tragedy. There were accidents and people died. (Private Collection.)

Three

FLYING DOWN TO RIO

Pan American's fleet of Sikorsky S-40 clippers flying over Miami provided a magnificent sight in January 1934. Described by none other than the *New York Times*, the S-40 was christened "America's mightiest airplane." Manufactured at Sikorsky's Bridgeport, Connecticut facility, workers turned out the S-40s as quickly as possible. *American Clipper*, accepted by Pan Am in October 1931, was followed by *Caribbean Clipper* in November 1931 and *Southern Clipper* in August 1932. The flying boats' interiors were magnificent; passenger compartments were paneled with top-quality walnut. There was four-abreast passenger seating and cabins appointed with blue carpeting and orange seat covers. The workhorses of Pan American's Caribbean network, the Sikorsky S-40s were worth their price for the airline. The flying boats were operated as passenger, training, or freighter aircraft until the early 1940s. They ended up as piles of scrapped trash in a Miami junkyard. (Florida State Archives.)

Speed, comfort, and excitement were promised in this advertisement, featuring the comfort of Consolidated Commodore and Sikorsky S-40 flying boats. After breakfast in Miami, passengers could "Travel the modern, colorful way—in liners of the air—huge multi-motored 'Clipper Ships,' the world's largest, finest—equipped with every facility for passenger comfort in constant radio communications—manned by veteran crews" and enjoy supper in Mexico, Jamaica, or Haiti. (Private Collection.)

In October 1928, Pan Am ceased operating out of Key West and moved its airline operation to Miami. Dedicated on September 15, 1929, the new terminal's interior featured prime examples of the Mediterranean Revival style of architecture so prevalent in Florida's boom-era construction. Located on Northwest Thirty-sixth Street, Pan American Field was situated on 116 acres and boasted a modern terminal building and three hangars. (Florida State Archives.)

Pan American announced plans in 1930 for the construction of a permanent passenger terminal at Dinner Key, Miami, Florida. On February 22, 1931, with great pomp and ceremony, Miami's mayor, C.H. Reeder, took part in official groundbreaking ceremonies by digging up the first spade full of dirt. While the terminal was under construction, the airline operated from a floating barge that had once been owned by New York, Rio, and Buenos Aires Line. (Private Collection.)

Constructed at a cost of several hundred thousand dollars, Pan American's Dinner Key facility was dedicated on March 24, 1934. Thousands turned out for the opening day celebration. The interior featured opulent waiting rooms, restaurants, and ticket counters. In its 15 years of airline operation from Dinner Key, Pan American made good use of the terminal; nearly 367,000 passengers flew in and out of Dinner Key. (Private Collection.)

NYRBA do Brasil, a subsidiary of New York, Rio and Buenos Aires Line, was part of the package Pan American acquired with the purchase of NYRBA in October 1929. The name of the Brazilian company was changed to Panair do Brasil on October 17, 1936. As the airline's name indicated, the company provided intra-Brazilian service only. Many of the advertisements for Pan American subsidiaries showed little variation in design, as indicated by this brochure and the next image, a baggage sticker for Panair do Brasil. The artwork, however, was always colorful and imaginative. Paintings and murals promoting the company decorated the walls of corporate offices, while hundreds of different designs advertised various entities within the company. Years after the demise of Pan Am, its travel posters, brochures, pamphlets, labels, and baggage stickers are highly collectible, as much for their artistic merit as their historical significance. (Private Collection.)

Critics of Juan Trippe and Pan American often claimed that Pan Am overcharged the United States Post Office. The argument may have had merit. While Pan Am charged the United States $2 per mile over several foreign airmail routes, Panair do Brasil charged the Brazilian government only 50¢ per pound. (Private Collection.)

Panair do Brasil operated Fairchild 91 Jungle Clipper amphibians on Brazil's 3,915-mile-long Amazon River. Manufactured by the Fairchild Aircraft Corporation of Hagerstown, Maryland, six Fairchild 91s were originally ordered by Panair do Brasil, each capable of carrying two crew members and eight passengers. Powered by a single 800-horsepower Pratt and Whitney Hornet engine, the Fairchild had a maximum speed of 170 miles per hour and a range of 700 miles. (Private Collection.)

GRANDE HOTEL

no roteiro dos
Clippers Voadores
da *PAA*

BELÉM
Pará, BRASIL

At Pan Am's destinations, the company either built or contracted for the operation of top-quality hotels. Passengers traveling to Belém, Brazil, the one-time rubber capital of the world, were treated to a stay at the Grande Hotel. Pan Am's "Around South America" brochure advertised, "Every night you enjoy the restful comfort of homelike beds and baths and the superlative hotel service of one of Pan American's famous airway inns." (Private Collection.)

ISTO É O BRASIL
II. O NORDESTE HERÓICO

PANAIR DO BRASIL

Pan American's advertising copywriters wrote magnificently flowery prose as an enticement to lure travelers onto its airplanes. This brochure touted "mountainous dunes of snow white sand rolling to the horizon, masses of jungle alive with orchids and tropical blossoms, groves of majestic coconut palms stretching for hundreds of miles." Who could read that description and resist dreaming about a trip to Brazil aboard a luxurious Pan American airplane? (Private Collection.)

A focal point of advertisements produced for not only Pan American, but also its South American subsidiaries Panair do Brasil, Mexicana, and Panagra, was a stylized four-engine Sikorsky S-40. The globe in the center was a frequent feature in Pan American advertising. As indicated by the white lines throughout the Caribbean and circling all of South America, Pan Am had a near monopoly on airline service in Latin America. (Private Collection.)

This advertisement pictured excited crowds preparing to board a Pan American Sikorsky S-40 at one of its American gateway cities. With its 1930s route system of nearly 30,000 miles, Pan Am offered dozens of Caribbean and South American destinations to both business and pleasure travelers. Only a few years hence, Trippe's route system would be expanded to include the continents of Asia and Europe. (Private Collection.)

Zoology students of the University of Miami used a Pan American 22-passenger Consolidated Commodore flying boat as a floating classroom. The 68-foot Commodore made an excellent portable floating pier for divers wishing to explore the depths of the Atlantic Ocean. The Commodore was originally designed by Consolidated for the United States Navy and designated the XPY-1. When the Glenn L. Martin Company ultimately underbid Consolidated for the

construction of the flying boat, Consolidated was left with designs and a prototype. Fortunately New York, Rio, and Buenos Aires Line purchased 14 of the flying boats. Thickly carpeted interiors and plush fabric upholstered seats offered state-of-the-art amenities to the traveling public. While the Commodore was a great improvement over the early Sikorskys, it was still not the aircraft that Juan Trippe wanted. (Florida State Archives.)

By the mid-1930s, the Consolidated Commodores acquired by Pan American in the acquisition of New York, Rio, and Buenos Aires Line were being phased out of the airline's fleet. The flying boats that had performed yeoman-like work were passé. Land planes had become more important than ever. By the end of 1934, Pan American's Latin American services were using 103 land airports and only 56 marine bases. (Florida State Archives.)

On November 30, 1932, Trippe signed contracts with the Glenn L. Martin Company and Sikorsky for development of a long-range flying boat. Trippe demanded that the aircraft have a range of 2,500 miles, a cruising speed of 155 miles per hour, and the ability to carry at least 16 people. Sikorsky took the S-40 and began improvements. Within a year, the first S-42 was finished; by December 1933, it was ready to fly. (Private Collection.)

In 1934, this Pan American timetable featuring a flying boat of indeterminate manufacture was printed entirely in Spanish and was distributed only in Mexico, Central America, and Cuba. Early on, Juan Trippe realized the power of national pride in Latin American countries. While Juan Trippe embraced a personal form of manifest destiny, he did not want host countries to feel that their larger North American neighbor had invaded them. (Private Collection.)

One more jewel in Trippe's crown of acquisition was Pan American-Grace (Panagra). The subsidiary came into being when it was formed on January 25, 1929, as an instrument to bid on FAM-9 from Panama to Argentina. When the airmail route was awarded to Panagra on March 9th, the company was incorporated a month later. Juan Trippe now had what he wanted—a route that completely circled South America. (Private Collection.)

In flight, the crew of a Sikorsky S-40 amphibian plotted a course from Miami to the Caribbean. The cockpit of the S-40 accommodated a crew of four including the captain, first officer, radio operator, and navigator. Outfitted in their blue uniforms and trademark white naval-style caps, Pan American crews portrayed competence and professionalism. Work rules were strict, almost as tight as in the military. Cigarette smoking while in uniform was strictly forbidden and was an

offense that would lead to instant termination. Pilots were rugged individualists, much like the earlier barnstormers; it had not been an easy task to mold them into a homogeneous work force. Although originally designed as an amphibian, the S-40 was retrofitted with 660-horsepower engines in 1935. With its landing gear removed, the S-40 was then a true flying boat. (Florida State Archives.)

Pan American spared no expense when it came to passenger amenities onboard its Sikorsky S-40s. This spacious teak-lined smoking compartment offered passengers the opportunity to relax, read, and enjoy light snacks. In order to reduce noise, the passenger compartments were carpeted; walls were lined with a blanket of insulation between the inner paneling and the aircraft's outer skin. (Florida State Archives.)

At Miami's Dinner Key facility, passengers prepared to board their clipper for a flight down to Rio. Prior to the flight, a steward passed out a small card with suggestions for enjoying the flight. It read in part, "Please see that your window is closed when taking off and landing. The Steward will hand you a small glassine envelope containing cotton and chewing gum. Place some cotton in your ears." (Florida State Archives.)

"Pan American to the Tropics" featured a Pan American Sikorsky S-42 flying boat. Pan American United States' gateway cities to the Caribbean and Latin America included Miami, Brownsville, El Paso, and Los Angeles. Printed in 1935, this brochure advertised the S-42 flying boats as ". . . aerial giants, whose four engines are more powerful than an average locomotive. Their dimensions are larger than ships in which Columbus first crossed the Atlantic. Their appointments are a revelation of what modern luxury can be. They carry a crew of five— Captain, Co-Pilot, Radio Operator, Flight Engineer, and Purser. Built for service over ocean waters these huge streamlined flying boats, weighing 17 and 19 tons, provide luxurious comfort for 32 and 40 passengers in cabins, each larger than a full size railroad car compartment, sound-proofed and automatically ventilated. Smoking compartments, promenade aisles 50 feet long, full-visioned windows, and a buffet from which luncheons and refreshments are served during flights are some of the unique features of these famous airliners." (Private Collection.)

Pan American relied heavily on Sikorsky aircraft in its advertising as evidenced by the S-42 on this brochure. The all-metal, high-wing Sikorsky S-42 monoplane was 68 feet in length, with a wing span of 118 feet. Four 750-horsepower Pratt and Whitney Hornet engines provided a cruising speed of over 160 miles per hour with a 1,200-mile range. The Sikorsky S-42 was a major departure from prior Sikorsky designs. Gone were the twin tail booms; there were also fewer wing struts. The engines no longer dangled from the wings but were aerodynamically set into wing nacelles. In 1934, the S-42, the most streamlined of all the Sikorsky flying boats produced, set ten flight performance records for speed, altitude, and weight carried. (Private Collection.)

Pan American's base radio station, WKDL, was located in Miami in 1936. Manned every hour of the day, radio operators kept track of Pan Am's aircraft during flight by radiotelegraph. Long before the days of portable and cellular phones, passengers could receive radiograms while on one of the airline's flights throughout the world. To insure the safety of the passengers, each of Pan American's operating fields boasted both radio transmitters and meteorological stations. Almost from the beginning of his operation, Juan Trippe believed in the use of radio as a means of aerial navigation. Pilots were extremely resistant at first, believing that an element of command was being taken from them and given to an unknown person on the ground. The pilots, however, eventually came to believe in the usefulness of radio navigation. Pan Am then was able to conquer the world. (Private Collection.)

Amelia Earhart, the world's best-known woman flier, was often seen at Pan American's Thirty-sixth Street airfield in Miami. A frequent visitor to Florida, she was also a regular participant in the All-American Air Maneuvers held annually in Miami. During her around-the-world flight, Earhart and Fred Noonan, her co-pilot/navigator, departed from Miami on June 1, 1937. Noonan had gained his flight experience as a navigator on Pan Am's *China Clipper*. On July 2nd, near Howland Island in the Pacific, Earhart transmitted a message to the U.S. Coast Guard ship *Itasca*. At 7:42 a.m. she radioed, "We must be on you but cannot see you but gas is running low." An hour later, all signals stopped. Earhart and Noonan were never heard from again. The most massive search ever formed was undertaken, but nothing was ever found. Nonetheless, Amelia Earhart will forever be the pilot against whom all female American pilots are judged. (Private Collection.)

Pan American's "Clipper Cruising" brochure offered 7,777 magical miles around the Caribbean Sea, the West Indies, South America, Central America, and Mexico. Travelers could now quickly travel to the "friendly continent of peaceful peoples, musical languages, romantic customs, thrilling history, striking beauty . . . where are found the world's greatest river, its highest continuous mountain range, its deepest jungle . . . whose eastern coast is serried with the world's most beautiful harbors and the great metropolises." (Private Collection.)

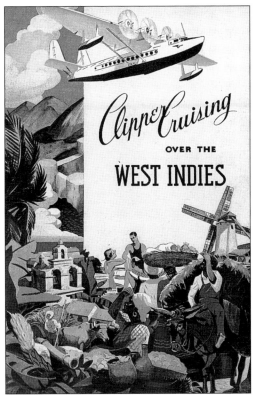

Inside this brochure, Pan Am's copywriters promised, "Where earthbound travelers must spend weeks to reach these interesting countries—and then catch but brief glimpses of their real charm—aerial voyagers explore their entire expanse in only two days." Where it once took days or even weeks to reach destinations such as Rio de Janeiro or Buenos Aires, the flying time was now only a few hours. (Private Collection.)

In 1936, a 12-day aerial clipper cruise from Miami to Rio de Janeiro cost $865. The cost of a 19-day trip to Rio de Janeiro, including a 10-day visit in Rio, was $895. Inside the brochure, Pan Am's advertising copy promised a traveler "10 countries along the way, 10,000 sights and sounds and experiences." The Sikorsky S-42 featured on the cover of this brochure was regarded as the most beautiful aircraft of its time. Following a rigorous program of testing by Captain Edwin C. Musick, Pan Am's chief pilot, and Boris Sergievsky, Sikorsky's test pilot, the sleek and aerodynamically pleasing S-42 was first used on Pan American's Latin American routes. Pan Am's first S-42, named *Brazilian Clipper*, made its maiden commercial flight on August 16, 1934, on the Miami-to-Rio de Janeiro route. The 32-passenger flying boat was later used to pioneer both transpacific and transatlantic routes. Over several years, Pan American used ten different models of the Sikorsky S-42 flying boats. (Private Collection.)

Four

CROSSING THE OCEANS

On November 22, 1935, more than 125,000 people witnessed the takeoff of a 25-ton Pan American Martin M-130 flying boat from San Francisco. History was being made; in less than a week, a person could cross the Pacific Ocean, the world's largest expanse of water, to the other side of the globe. After overnight stops at Honolulu, Midway, Wake, and Guam, the *China Clipper* arrived in the Philippines. Following 60 hours of flying on a trip that took 6 days, 7 hours, and 46 minutes of elapsed time, the *China Clipper* was met by more than 250,000 people as it landed at Manila Bay on November 29. To Captain Edwin Musick went the honor of personally delivering a letter from President Franklin D. Roosevelt to Manuel L. Quezon, president of the Commonwealth of the Philippines. The first transpacific flight carried a cargo of 111,000 letters. The entire world had followed the preparations, as almost every newspaper covered the story. The *New York World-Telegram* had done a series of 11 articles on the preparations for the crossing of the Pacific. (Private Collection.)

Hundreds of boats in Manila Bay surrounded the 25-ton Martin flying boat, the *China Clipper*, shortly after its arrival in the Philippines. As the Filipino Constabulary band played, approximately 250,000 people watched the 91-foot-long Martin taxi to a mooring at Admirals Landing in front of the Manila Hotel. On the first airmail flight across the Pacific, Musick's flight crew included five transport pilots, three aeronautical engineers, three licensed radio operators, and two master mariners. (Private Collection.)

The people of the Philippines welcomed the *China Clipper*'s crew following completion of the first scheduled airmail flight. In a short speech, Musick told the enthusiastic crowd, "Today's flight is not the result of a simple process. Five years of ceaseless planning, designing and construction, training and practice have advanced aviation to this point where today it is possible for us to span an ocean." (Private Collection.)

Known as "meticulous Musick" by Pan Am's pilots, Captain Edwin Musick had been flying for 22 years. Although laconic and publicity-shy after his conquest of the Pacific Ocean by air, Musick was unable to escape the press. One of the world's most experienced airmen, it was estimated that he had actually spent almost five years in the air. On January 11, 1938, while on a route-proving flight for service to New Zealand, Musick's aircraft developed engine trouble shortly after takeoff from Pago Pago. Needing to reduce the aircraft's weight before landing, Musick gave the order to dump fuel. The *Samoan Clipper* exploded. At the age of only 42, Pan Am's chief pilot Edwin Musick perished along with six crewmen in the fiery crash of his Sikorsky S-42B. The next day, rescuers located only oil slicks and floating debris; the cause remained a mystery. Trippe was forced to temporarily suspend Pan Am's South Pacific service. (Private Collection.)

Twenty-five years after the 1935 flight across the Pacific Ocean, Filipino President Ramon Magsaysay awarded Juan Trippe the Medal of the Legion of Honor. Magsaysay cited Trippe and Pan American for "Materially contributing to the establishment of closer ties between the Philippines and the United States, particularly in the reduction of travel time to a matter of only a few hours." (Private Collection.)

When Pan Am pioneered air routes across the Pacific Ocean, it was necessary to build remote bases for refueling stops. Gooney birds roosted on the lawn in front of the Pan American Hotel on Midway Island. The first commercial transpacific flight took less than a week. The planning and preparation had taken five years. Pan Am had begun surveying routes to the Orient in 1931. (Private Collection.)

Pan Am crewmen come ashore at Midway Island, located in the Pacific Ocean 1,304 miles from Honolulu. In preparation for its Pacific expansion, Pan American began working on its bases in the Pacific Ocean in 1935. Since the 8,200-mile trip across the Pacific took five days, the journey required overnight and refueling stops. On March 27, 1935, a cargo ship, the *North Haven*, left San Francisco. Loaded with construction supplies, water, fuel, furniture, and food, it was bound for Honolulu, Midway, Wake, Guam, and Manila. Complete flying bases were constructed and equipped for the first time at Midway, Wake, and Guam, while existing bases at Honolulu were reinforced. (Private Collection.)

In preparation for the establishment of a commercial route across the Pacific Ocean, Pan American survey flights began in 1935. A specially outfitted Sikorsky S-42 had been stripped of all amenities in order to add extra fuel tanks. Although the smell of aviation fuel was constant, the changes allowed a range of 3,000 miles and almost 22 hours of flying time. On April 16, 1935, the plane carrying Captain Edwin Musick and his five crewmen lifted off the water near San Francisco headed for Honolulu, a distance of almost 2,000 miles. Their flight was perfect, taking only 18 hours and 37 minutes. Four days later, the crew returned to San Francisco. In an interview upon arrival, Musick told reporters, "I think this flight has removed the element of chance on the trans-Pacific journey." That was not the case, however. On April 22nd, a Pan Am S-42 arrived in San Francisco after a flight of 23 hours and 41 minutes. Immediately following takeoff, heavy headwinds had greatly reduced their speed. For a time, the crew had been lost and the aircraft had nearly run out of fuel. (Private Collection.)

CHINA CLIPPER

Pan American inaugurated weekly regularly scheduled passenger service between New York's Port Washington and Bermuda on June 18, 1937. Using 32-seat Sikorsky S-42 flying boats, the weekly service quickly expanded to twice a week. Service was soon added between Baltimore and Bermuda. The operation provided important experience with the unique weather and flight problems inherent in Atlantic flying. (Florida State Archives.)

Pan American's 1936 timetable promised "a smaller world than ever," as evidenced by the company's destinations. While China was last on the list, its importance could not be underestimated from a social standpoint. A contemporary travel publication believed, "Only by numbers of Americans visiting China, and seeing for themselves the mighty things accomplished by the ancient Chinese, will America ever obtain the full benefits which Chinese philosophy can give it." (Private Collection.)

Pan American's sea and air cruises to the Orient offered a transportation combination featuring both steamer and airplane flights. Round-trip service between San Francisco and Shanghai cost $1,483. Vacationing or business travelers took a steamer to Honolulu, followed by a Pan American clipper flight to one of several Pacific destinations. The flights on board the large Martin M-130 flying boats were luxurious. Well-trained and attentive stewards saw to the every need of their passengers. Little expense was spared on passenger amenities; meals served on board were freshly prepared and served on tables covered with linen. Each night, as the trip progressed, the passengers would sleep in one of the Pan American hotels at the overnight stops of Midway, Wake, Guam, or Manila. While the crew and passengers slept, Pan Am mechanics cleaned the cabins and made sure the flying boat was ready to go. After breakfast, passengers would board the Martin flying boat and fly to the next intermediate stop. (Private Collection.)

DOMAIN OF PHOEBUS

Ruler of the Sun and Heavens

INTERNATIONAL DATE LINE

Pacific Ocean

SAN FRANCI

MIDWAY

HONGKONG
MACAO
MANILA

WAKE

HONOLULU

GUAM

Trans Pacific Route
PAN AMERICA
AIRWAYS SYSTE

Know All Peoples

That _H. G. Gulbransen_ , once earthbound and time-laden,

Sun and of the Heavens, with the freedom of our Sacred Eagle..... That with the speed of Our

skies over the International Date Line, which mortals designed to mark off in the limit of days Our Ete

crossing this divider of days between the earth isles of Midway and Wake, the Today of mortals at o

That this subject is commanded to hold ever close this Celestial Decree so that in the final accounting

Done in the Realm of the Sun and of the Heavens by the order of Phoebus Apollo,

Aboard _China Clipper_ _9-44 a.m_ _November 29-30, 19_

Time of Crossing

ared a subject of the *Realm* of the
Chariot this subject did fly the *Pacific*
c through the skies..... *That* by so
Tomorrow and all is confusion.....
days, the balance will stand true.....
of *Zeus* and *Leto.*
Miller Captain.
alisary Plenipotentiary

Pan American's clipper passengers became subjects of "the Realm of the Sun and of the Heavens, with the freedom of our Sacred Eagle," when they crossed the international dateline at a spot "between the earth isles of Midway and Wake." As the Pan American clipper reached the dateline, 200 miles west of Midway, a member of the crew walked through the cabin, distributing the "Celestial Decrees" to the passengers. The blue-and-gold dateline certificate showed the passenger's name, the name of the aircraft, and the date of crossing. According to the document, ". . . the Today of mortals at once becomes Tomorrow and all is confusion . . ." In the southern hemisphere, passengers crossing the Equator on a Pan American flight were given membership in the "Order of Jupiter Rex." (Private Collection.)

Almost a year after the inauguration of service from the United States to Manila, Pan Am was ready to complete the route into Hong Kong. On October 21, 1936, the *Philippine Clipper* departed Honolulu. The *Philippine Clipper,* the second of three Martin M-130s acquired by Pan American, arrived in Hong Kong Harbor on October 23rd. Pan Am had established the first commercial air link between North America and the Asian continent. (Private Collection.)

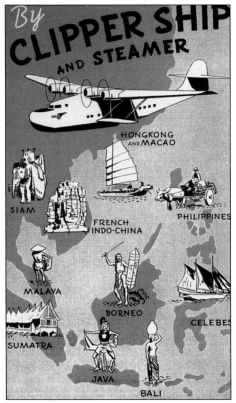

Pan American flights to exotic Asian destinations promised romance and mystery. In concert with steamship, rail, and motor lines, travel was at a leisurely pace, sometimes taking months. Pan Am advertising declared, "Whether you wish to be gone a week or a year—or whether you wish to vagabond as fancy dictates, the luxurious, frequent, and dependable services of Pan American Airways system offer you a new experience in travel." (Private Collection.)

During the 19th century, legendary American sailing ships such as *Red Jacket, Eagle, Live Yankee, Flying Cloud,* and *Young America* became a symbol of American seamanship. Like the sleek clipper sailing ships of an earlier era, Juan Trippe and Pan American's aircraft mastered time and distance to make the world smaller and bring the diverse people of the world ever closer together. On October 12, 1931, Mrs. Herbert Hoover, wife of the president of the United States, smashed a bottle of Caribbean water against the hull of a Sikorsky S-40 flying boat. Twelve thousand people watched the ceremony as U.S. Navy and Marine bands played the national anthem. The flying boat was christened *Clipper America,* thus beginning a tradition of naming Pan American aircraft after famous American clipper sailing ships. In years to come, each Pan American aircraft would be named as a clipper; different kinds of aircraft would be assigned a particular clipper type. Birds, patriotic themes, seas and oceans, celestial bodies, and categories of people such as gladiators or archers provided sources for names. (Private Collection.)

As much as Trippe wanted to conquer the Pacific Ocean, he also desired operating rights within the huge country of China. It was not about to happen. Fearful that the Japanese would demand the same rights, General Chiang Kai-Shek would not permit it. Trippe dealt with the problem by buying 45 percent ownership in the China National Aviation Corporation (CNAC), which had been originally founded by the Curtiss-Wright Corporation in 1929. (Private Collection.)

On March 31, 1933, a contract was signed with the Chinese government giving Pan American partial ownership of China National Aviation Corporation. Scheduled service along China's coast began on October 23rd. CNAC operated from Peiping in the north along the coast to Canton in the south and west to Chunking. Bad weather and fear of Japanese attacks made the flights difficult for the American and Chinese crews. (Private Collection.)

PAA PAN AMERICAN WORLD AIRWAYS

CLIPPER TRAVEL

NAME _____

HOME ADDRESS _____

DESTINATION _____

HOTEL _____ ROOM NO: _____

Pan American Clipper Travel baggage tags insured that luggage and passengers reached the same destination. The airline's free baggage allowance was 77 pounds, the equivalent of two large bags. Additional baggage could be carried for a nominal excess baggage charge. Advertising literature stated that the fact that passengers would be "with new and different groups every few days, voids the need for an extensive wardrobe." (Private Collection.)

CLIPPER AIR CHEQUES

For the Convenience of Travelers via

PAN AMERICAN AIRWAYS SYSTEM

Issued by

AMERICAN EXPRESS COMPANY

In the 1940s, for the convenience of its passengers, Pan American sold Clipper Air Cheques through worldwide American Express company offices. Almost from the airline's inception, travel companies such as American Express and Thomas Cook had been a major help in the marketing of Pan American. Their agents were able to provide Pan Am passengers with necessary health requirements and assist with the acquisition of required visas and passports. (Private Collection.)

MACAO
Earliest "doorway" into China, Macao was established by the Portuguese in 1557—one of the most picturesque of old world ports.

HONG KONG

PHILIPPINE ISLANDS
Discovered by Magellan in 1542; Annexed to Spain in 1865; Ceded to U. S. in 1898. Won status of Commonwealth, 1935.
Distance: From Guam 1,587 miles
From Honolulu 6,345 miles
From California 7,990 miles
To Hong Kong 759 miles

GUAM
Discovered by Magellan, 1521; Called "Lateen Sails Island" because of the soil rig of native canoes. Possessed by Spain, 1565; Ceded to U. S. in 1898.
Latitude: 13° 26' North
Longitude: 144° 40' East
Distance: From Wake 1,508 miles

WAKE ISLAND
Discovered in 1796; Charted by Wilkes in 1841; Possessed for U. S. in 1899; First Colonized in 1935 by Pan American Airways.
Latitude: 9° 19' North
Longitude: 166° 36' East
Time change: from California: 5 hours.
Date change: One day
Distance from: California 4,893 miles;

In opening up global air service across the Pacific Ocean, Pan American proved the value of long-distance air transportation. As evidenced by this graphic of Pan Am's Pacific service, travel that once required weeks by ocean-going vessel was reduced to only a few days. Trippe's vision included more than the carrying of passengers. To make the Pacific routes cost-effective, the airline had to aggressively market mail and express package service. As an unofficial instrument

72

MIDWAY ISLANDS
...laimed for the U. S. in 1859;
...onized 1902; Present Population, 44.
...atitude: 28° 13' North
...ongitude: 177° 27' West
...ance from Hololulu: 1,304 miles
California: 3,703 miles
...change from California: 4 hours.

HAWAIIAN ISLANDS
Discovered by Captain James Cook, in 1778, and
originally called the Sandwich Islands. Largest group
in the Central Pacific, the island chain reaches over
1,500 miles. A native kingdom, until 1819, then a re-
public until the group became a Territory of the
United States in 1898 by voluntary annexation. Semi-

SAN FRANCISCO TO HAWAII
Distance: 2,404 miles;   Time: ove...
Time change from California: 2½ ho...

At San Francisco, direct connections are made w...
Lines—and at Los Angeles, with American Airli...
continental—Western Air—for through overni...

of the American government, Pan American received a great deal of assistance from the United
States Navy in the development of the necessary operating bases throughout the Pacific Ocean.
Juan Trippe concluded a speech by saying, "This world of ours, in the age of flight, should be
one world." Both he and the U.S. government obviously envisioned it as an American world.
(Private Collection.)

In the early 1940s, Pan Am used a foldout brochure to tout its foreign vacations and its service to several countries. Pan Am encouraged travelers on board a flying clipper to "Go air cruising to Mexico—Guatemala. Wing away to the West Indies. Bermuda five hours by clipper. Alaska by air. Tour historic Peru or dazzling Rio, and see all South America by air." (Private Collection.)

After receiving authorization in 1937 to fly to Bermuda, Pan Am began making preparations for New York to Bermuda service. Using Sikorsky S-42B flying boats, Pan American pilots made several survey flights to Bermuda in May. Pan Am inaugurated regular once-a-week passenger service over the 775-mile route between Port Washington, New York, and Hamilton, Bermuda, on June 18, 1937. Weekly service quickly expanded to twice a week. (Private Collection.)

The round-trip fare in November 1937 for the five-hour flight from New York to Bermuda was ___. In addition to the New York service, flights were added in November between Baltimore and Bermuda, using S-42Bs and Boeing 314s. The Bermuda operation provided important experience with the unique weather and flight problems inherent in Atlantic flying. (Private Collection.)

Twenty-two passengers, including six women, prepared to board their silver-and-orange Pan Am clipper for the first commercial flight across the Atlantic Ocean on June 28, 1939. Of the $375 one-way fare, Pan Am's chairman of the board Cornelius V. Whitney said, "For a trip of this kind, that is moderate. We have tried to place it at a level within the reach of businessmen and all travelers who wish to use this type of high-speed transportation to Europe." (Private Collection.)

The *Dixie Clipper*, Pan American's giant 42-ton Boeing 314 flying boat, took off on Long Island Sound, New York. Commanded by Captain R.O.D. Sullivan, the highly experienced crew of 12 had logged thousands of hours of flying time. The history-making flight to Marseilles, France, took 29 hours and 20 minutes to complete, with stops in the Azores and Lisbon. Cruising at a speed of 150 miles per hour, the needs of the 22 passengers were taken care of by well-trained

stewards. For the trip, a Long Island restaurant had prepared the meals, including a complete selection of wines and liquors. Meal service included a formal table setting with china embossed with the Pan American logo. One of the two stewards on the flight recalled, "It was the last word in luxury for its day." (Private Collection.)

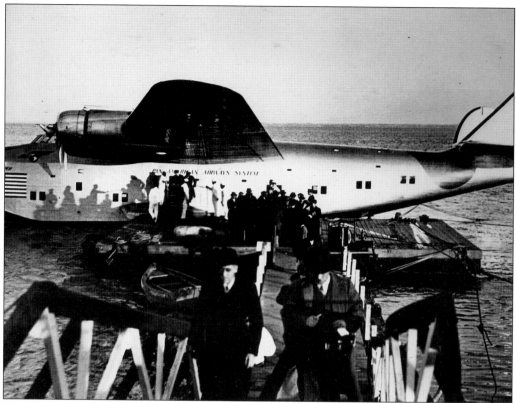

The first passengers to cross the Atlantic by air are shown disembarking from the *Dixie Clipper* at Lisbon, Portugal, at 2:20 p.m. on June 29, 1939. Less than 23 hours after leaving New York, the Pan Am clipper had touched down in the harbor of Horta, the Azores. By 8:05 p.m., they were moored at Lisbon. The next day, the Pan Am flight arrived at Marseilles, France. History had been made. (Private Collection.)

The *Atlantic Clipper*, shown moored at Miami's Dinner Key terminal, had been extensively used on Pan American's transatlantic and transpacific routes. The aircraft came to a tragic end in February 1943 when it crashed at Lisbon, Portugal. Civil Aeronautics Board technicians found Robert Oliver Daniel Sullivan, captain of the *Atlantic Clipper*, responsible for the crash. With over 14,000 flying hours to his credit, Sullivan was forced to leave Pan Am in disgrace. (Florida State Archives.)

Pan American began transatlantic airmail service on May 20, 1939, with service from New York to Marseilles, France. Captain Mike La Porte, a veteran of 50 Pacific crossings, was at the controls of the Boeing 314. When questioned by reporters, he said that although it was "fine to be on the first flight, this is pretty much a routine operation of the line." Following takeoff, La Porte radioed, "We are proceeding to Europe." (Private Collection.)

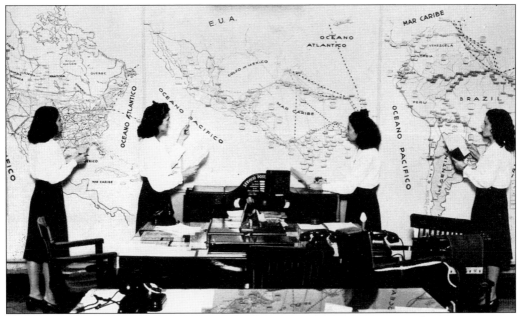

Women long played an important role in Pan American's success. Passenger service representatives kept track of reservations, routes, and plane connections. In addition to a world map, the office featured floor-to-ceiling boards on either side of the room. Marked in squares delineating flight numbers and dates, the boards used color coding to indicate flight status. A red "X" in a square showed that the flight was sold out. (Private Collection.)

Pan Am's September 1940 timetable boasted that airmail service was 30 times faster than ordinary mail. The carriage of mail and express packages was a financial windfall for Pan Am. Pan Am marketing literature claimed that by using Pan Am's airmail service, businesses could speed up their foreign trade by 300 percent. Within two years of the opening of Pacific and European service, Pan Am doubled the amount of mail it carried. (Private Collection.)

By 1943, Pan American clippers had flown more than 285 million miles of over-ocean flight. Trippe's airline circled the globe, except for a short route between Singapore and the Middle East. In his office located on the 58th floor of New York City's Chrysler Building, Trippe kept a large globe and a ball of string used to plan out new routes for his airline. (Private Collection.)

Five

WORLD'S MOST EXPERIENCED AIRLINE

As Pan American prepared to enter the 1940s, the airline industry and the world were in a state of flux. While war raged in Europe, Juan Trippe prepared to move his company into a new age of technology. The flying boats that had allowed Pan Am to circle South America and conquer the Pacific and Atlantic Oceans were being phased out in favor of four-engine, pressurized land planes capable of high-altitude flights at great speeds. Trippe continued to raise money through stock issues; the new Boeing and Douglas airplanes were costly. The decade of the 1930s had been characterized by great expansion through internal growth and acquisition of other airlines. Pan American had been a pioneer in not only the development of new routes but also in pushing aircraft manufacturers to build bigger and faster aircraft. In 1940, Pan Am carried 6 million pounds of freight. Within a few short years, that number would increase ten-fold. Juan Trippe's Pan American Airways had become a symbol of America around the world. (Private Collection.)

The flight deck of one of over 13,000 Douglas DC-3s manufactured for foreign and domestic airlines was far more sophisticated than that of its predecessors. Although American Airlines was the launch operator on the 21-passenger DC-3, Pan American made good use of the aircraft. Powered by a pair of Pratt and Whitney engines, the DC-3 boasted a cruising speed of 180 miles per hour and a 500-mile range. (Florida State Archives.)

The venerated Douglas DC-3 was used by Pan American and every other airline in the 1930s and 1940s. The 64-foot-long DC-3 was also operated by several of Pan American's subsidiaries, including Panair do Brasil, SCADTA, Mexicana, and CNAC. During World War II, the DC-3 was used on Pan American's Alaskan service, as well as by CNAC to fly supplies over the "Hump" between India and China. (Private Collection.)

Flying boats such as this would soon be a thing of the past. In March 1937, Pan American Airways ordered its first four-engine, pressurized land plane, the Boeing S-307, popularly known as the Stratoliner. After a three-year wait, Pan Am placed the first of its three Stratoliners into service. On June 3, 1940, a Pan Am S-307 made its inaugural scheduled flight with service to Bogota, Colombia, followed by flights to several other South American cities. (Florida State Archives.)

Boeing manufactured only ten of the Stratoliners. Trans World Airlines (TWA) purchased seven, while the other three went to Pan Am. The 33-passenger airplane was used primarily on Pan American's Alaskan service as well as in Central and South America. Not yet capable of nonstop transoceanic service, the Boeing S-307 was of great importance; the Stratoliner allowed the airline to fly above the weather and give passengers a smooth and safe flight. (Private Collection.)

Pan American founded its subsidiary, Pan American Airways-Africa Ltd., to provide route facilities and transport service for the delivery of lend-lease cargo and the return of ferry pilots. The task was quickly accomplished. In a two-month period, Pan American Airways-Africa had constructed or improved airports at Dakar, Accra, Lagos, Kano, Maiduguri, El Geneina, El Fasher, and Khartoum. Pan American Air Ferries was incorporated on July 24, 1941. (Private Collection.)

A group of Hudson bombers and B-26s sat on the tarmac at Pan American's Miami facility in 1942. During World War II, Pan Am crews ferried thousands of lend-lease aircraft for the Allies. Pan Am's Africa-Orient Division was one of the company's busiest divisions. Out of Miami and New York bases, Pan Am flew in excess of 2 million miles each month. Each day, under the direction of the Army Transport Command, Pan Am's airplanes made 13 Atlantic crossings. (Private Collection.)

A Catalina PBY-5A amphibian being delivered by a crew from Pan American Air Ferries crashed on takeoff at Eritrea on October 31, 1942. Overloading was the cause of the accident. Incorporated on July 24, 1941, Trippe's subsidiary was, for the most part, crewed by pilots that were too old to fly for the military or the airline. Each day, ferry pilots transported aircraft south to South America and across the Atlantic to Africa. (Private Collection.)

Wings Over the World, Pan Am's 1942 annual report, was reviewed by the Office of Censorship. Certain detailed information regarding routes, operations, and passenger traffic was omitted in the interest of national security. Two years later, in the 1944 report, Juan Trippe wrote, "Ninety of the System's personnel have given their lives in performance of their duties during the war period. Forty-five are still interned in Japanese prison camps." (Private Collection.)

**PAN AMERICAN
WORLD AIRWAYS SYSTEM**

ANNUAL REPORT FOR THE WAR YEAR
1942

Neophyte Army Air Forces navigators marched to class at Pan American's Dinner Key facility. At the request of the military, Pan American established a navigation school in Miami. In these "flying classrooms," Pan Am instructors taught Army, Navy, British, and Canadian prospective navigators the intricacies of in-flight navigation. Each year during the war, Pan American trained approximately 1,000 military navigators in a 350-hour course. With the Japanese attack on Pearl Harbor in the Pacific on December 7, 1941, Pan American became part of the war. Japanese fighters at Hong Kong destroyed a Pan Am Sikorsky S-42B flying boat named the *Clipper Hong Kong*. Stations on Pan Am's main Pacific route were also destroyed by the Japanese air attack. As quickly as possible, over half of Pan Am's equipment had been painted a dull sea-gray and was serving the war effort. (Florida State Archives.)

≋NEW≋
HORIZONS
THE MAGAZINE OF AMERICA'S MERCHANT MARINE OF THE AIR

Bachrach

PRESIDENT J. T. TRIPPE
He led off a 3-star procession
(THE MONTH)

During World War II, Trippe wrote, "On behalf of the war effort, Pan American Airways has been privileged to undertake assignments which the President of the United States has characterized as of an importance which cannot be overestimated." Shortly after the United States entered the war, attempts were made to entice Trippe to command a military air transport command. He rejected the offer, preferring to continue as chairman of his airline. The routes of America's domestic airlines hardly changed during World War II. For Pan Am, an international airline with routes in South America, the Pacific, and Europe, things were obviously different. Pan American unarguably made a contribution to victory during World War II. In 1944 alone, Pan American pilots flew 80 million miles, "equivalent to more than 3,000 times around the world—an average of more than 17 over-ocean flights a day, a total of 6,240 for the year. Nearly half of those miles were under contract for the Army and Navy." (Private Collection.)

Pan Am carried thousands of political and military dignitaries on its flights throughout World War II. Aboard a Pan Am clipper on January 30, 1943, President Franklin D. Roosevelt returned from Casablanca, Morocco, where he had been a participant in the Casablanca Conference. Winston Churchill, Queen Wilhelmina of the Netherlands, and King George of Greece were also passengers on one of over 700 special missions flown by Pan Am. (Private Collection.)

During World War II, Pan American's subsidiary, China National Aviation Corporation, was a major force in the Burma-China "Hump" operation. This CNAC DC-3 airplane, with a cannibalized DC-2 wing, was a sight seldom seen. The route between India and China was one of the most dangerous trips flown by pilots. To keep the lifeline open, pilots braved 20,000-foot mountain peaks, horrible weather, and Japanese fighters. (Private Collection.)

"you buy 'em we'll fly 'em!"

Wilkinsons

DEFENSE BONDS STAMPS

Pan American personnel around the world enthusiastically embraced the message of this patriotic war bond poster. Men and women throughout the Pan Am system frequently pooled their funds and purchased war bonds. Some went beyond the call of duty; the *Africa-Orient Clipper* reported that 13 maintenance men stationed at Natal had bought $4,700 worth of bonds in the company's fifth war bond drive. (Private Collection.)

Many of Pan Am's flights during World War II were into war zones, and at times, they were under fire from enemy guns. Cargoes carried were varied. Preparing to board a Pan Am flight for a USO tour are, from left to right, Tony Romano, Jerry Colonna, Vera Vagne, Wendell Niles, Frances Langford, and Bob Hope. On most of their flights, Pan Am carried thousands of pounds of V-mail for the troops. (Private Collection.)

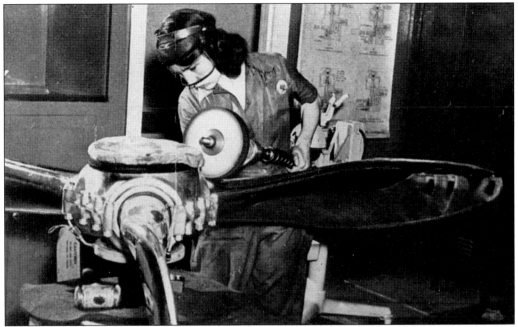

Audrey Steel, a Pan Am mechanic's helper at La Guardia Field, buffed a 435-pound propeller to a mirror shine with care and precision. Propellers were pulled off airplanes and reconditioned at prescribed intervals. Pan Am employed almost 200 women as mechanic's helpers at La Guardia Field in New York and just as many at its Miami facilities. (Private Collection.)

During World War II, Judy Moulton was assigned as an instructor at the Pan American navigation school in Miami. She held the distinction of being the only female celestial navigation instructor in the world. Each day, in a very nontraditional role, Moulton passed her skills on to potential military and airline navigators at Pan Am's Dinner Key facility. (Private Collection.)

As the war neared an end, Pan American began planning for its future, which included orders for postwar transport airplanes. The goal of Juan T. Trippe and Pan American was to ". . . make possible low fares which in turn will make worldwide airborne mass transportation a reality for the average American and his family." Soon the flying boats that had conquered oceans would be a thing of the past. (Private Collection.)

With World War II over, people were ready for pleasure travel. Along with flights and tour packages, Pan American offered a network of quality hotels and guest houses throughout South America. Due to the costs of expansion and the purchase of new equipment, most airlines lost money. With Juan Trippe at its helm, Pan American was one of the few exceptions. (Private Collection.)

Pan American entered the hotel business at the request of the United States government, which believed that quality hotels in Latin America would serve to improve relations. In 1946, the Inter-Continental Hotel chain was incorporated. Its first property was a hotel in Belem, Brazil, which offered—of all things—air conditioning. The company would eventually own or manage over 75 hotels in 50 countries. (Private Collection.)

In 1940, Trippe ordered 20 Lockheed L-49 Constellations. The airline would not receive the "Connies" until the war ended. Almost since the beginning of Pan Am, Trippe had envisioned one-airline-round-the-world service. On June 17, 1947, a Pan Am Lockheed L-49 departed La Guardia Airport with Trippe and several newspaper publishers. Two weeks later, they were back in the United States. Pan Am had made the first scheduled round-the-world flight. (Private Collection.)

Approximately 15,000 people turned out at the Miami airport in 1949 to inspect the newest airplane in Pan American's fleet—the Boeing Stratocruiser. During the two-day celebration, Margaret Truman, daughter of President Harry Truman, christened the Stratocruiser *Clipper America*. Pan Am bought a total of 20 Stratocruisers, described by many aviation historians as one of the most comfortable airplanes ever built. The perfect airplane for transatlantic travel, its comfort was obvious; it featured a double-decker fuselage that offered berths, staterooms, sumptuous dining, five flight attendants, and a lower-level lounge. First ordered in late 1945, Pan Am placed its first Stratocruiser into service between San Francisco and Honolulu on April 1, 1949. Within a few months, the Stratocruisers had been further incorporated into the Pan Am system, flying New York to Bermuda and New York to London. (Florida State Archives.)

Powered by four Pratt and Whitney engines, Pan American's 60-passenger Boeing Stratocruisers offered a 3,000-mile range at cruising speeds of 300 miles per hour. The 110-foot-long Stratocruiser was a derivative of the United States Air Force B-29 Super Fortress. Redesigned as the military KC-97 tanker transport, the aircraft eventually entered airline service as the Boeing Stratocruiser. (Private Collection.)

A pair of American Overseas Airlines' Stratocruisers are painted in Pan Am's colors of blue and white. Trippe targeted American Overseas, an American Airlines' subsidiary, as a candidate for merger in December 1948. When the merger was disapproved by the Civil Aviation Board in 1950, President Harry Truman reversed the decision. Pan Am received an up-to-date fleet of Stratocruisers, Constellations, DC-4s, and 2,500 new route miles. (Florida State Archives.)

The globe with eagle's wings was an early symbol of Pan American and its clippers. As the war ended, Pan Am emerged as by far the largest of all American-owned airlines. Now Trippe was looking for mergers, new aircraft, and domestic routes. On August 1, 1950, the Civil Aviation Board denied Pan American's request for domestic routes, making Pan Am destined to be an international airline only. (Private Collection.)

A newly hired Pan American flight attendant proudly poses in her uniform. When women were finally hired as flight attendants, a typical advertisement for an airline "hostess" read, "Registered nurses, age 21 to 26, height 5 feet 2 inches to 5 feet 5 inches, weight 100 to 125 pounds." Flight attendants earned from $125 to $200 a month. (Private Collection.)

Throughout its years of corporate life, Pan Am operated under several names, such as Pan American Airways, Inc. and Pan American Airways System. By the mid-1940s, Trippe's airline had become Pan American World Airways. In the early 1950s, a series of labels commemorating its worldwide service were printed. The airline had evolved from a fleet of flying boats over a mostly North and South American route structure to a worldwide network featuring state-of-

the-art land planes. With World War II becoming a distant memory, Trippe prepared to take the company to new heights. Pan Am boasted nearly 20,000 employees and revenues of $250 million. Trippe jettisoned the men that had helped him make Pan Am what it was. Employees unionized; pilots belonged to the Airline Pilots Association, while clerical employees joined the Brotherhood of Railroad Clerks. (Private Collection.)

A Pan Am Boeing Stratocruiser awaits attention in one of the hangars at Pan Am's Miami maintenance complex. In 1949, the airline produced a multipage brochure presenting the history and development of this airplane, described as "the fastest, most luxurious airliner ever built." André Priester, Pan Am's chief engineer, personally took delivery of the company's first Stratocruiser from William M. Allen, president of the Boeing Airplane Company, on January 31, 1949. (Florida State Archives.)

Airplanes lined the ramp at Pan Am's Miami maintenance facility. With the introduction of Douglas DC-6 and DC-7 aircraft to the fleet, the airline greatly increased available seats, as well as the range and speed of its fleet. Pan Am inaugurated 82-passenger DC-6 service from New York to London on May 1, 1952. On June 13, 1955, the 353-mile-per-hour DC-7B began flying the same route. (Florida State Archives.)

Six

THE JET AGE

Pan American World Airways became the unchallenged leader over the North Atlantic with the use of the four-engine Boeing 707. Juan Trippe used Charles Lindbergh as his point man on the transition into jets, after Lindbergh visited the Boeing facility and came away satisfied that a jet transport was the way to go. Boeing was working on its own version that would eventually be known as the 707. Douglas was designing its own jet aircraft, the DC-8. Trippe, almost single-handedly, was responsible for the first jet transport capable of crossing the Atlantic Ocean nonstop. Through his foresight and refusal to give up, the redesign of the engines and airplane allowed just such a feat. Pan Am had frequently been Boeing's lead customer; it was now the same with the 707. Pan Am wanted the 707, and Boeing would build it. Playing Boeing and Douglas against the other, Trippe signed a contract with both airline manufacturers on the same day. (Private Collection.)

Spend more time
at your destination

than ever before!

Flying at 600 miles per hour, Jet Clippers will get you there almost twice as fast as piston-engined aircraft . . . more than 30% faster than turbo-propeller planes!

See how much faster you can fly
NEW YORK TO EUROPE

JET CLIPPER ✈ 6½ HRS.

TURBO-PROP ✈ 9½ HRS.

PISTON ✈ 11 HRS.

Most planes in commercial airline service today are piston-engined aircraft, although a few airlines now operate turbo-*prop*-powered planes. Turbo-propeller aircraft do have some speed advantage over piston-engine planes; but they are not pure jets, they still depend on the propellers for propulsion.

Pan Am's new Jet Clippers — Boeing 707's and Douglas DC-8's soon to be delivered — will offer the finest, fastest service. No increase in the new transatlantic *economy* class fares. You will have the most relaxing and refreshing trip of your life. And you'll step from your Jet Clipper alert and ready for either vacation pleasures or business conferences.

PAN AMERICAN JET CLIPPERS

NOW TO EUROPE . . . SOON THROUGHOUT THE WORLD!

Clipper, Trade-Mark Reg. U.S. Pat. Off.
Copyright, 1958 Pan American World Airways, Inc.

In accordance with the contracts, Boeing would provide small 707s not suitable for transatlantic flights; Douglas would build wider and larger DC-8s capable of transoceanic travel. Because of the competing Douglas airplane, Boeing was forced to redesign their 707, making it longer and wider than planned and powered by engines capable of transoceanic flight. It was what Trippe wanted from the beginning—an airplane that would greatly reduce transatlantic flight time. (Private Collection.)

On October 26, 1958, Juan Trippe's Pan American World Airways entered the jet age when it inaugurated Boeing 707 service from New York's Idlewild Airport to Paris with *Clipper America*. Captain Samuel Hudson Miller, chief pilot for Pan Am in 1958, recalled that compared to propeller airplanes, the four-engine jet-powered Boeing 707 "was like getting out of a Model T and stepping into an air-conditioned Rolls Royce." (Private Collection.)

On July 2, 1962, Pan Am operated its 100,000th transatlantic flight. Since Pan Am's first transatlantic flight in 1939, the airline had carried almost 3.6 million passengers to destinations in Europe and Great Britain. Captain Robert D. Fordyce was in command of *Clipper America*, the 707 being used to celebrate the historic feat. Fordyce had served as a junior flight officer 23 years earlier on Pan Am's first transatlantic passenger flight. (Private Collection.)

Kenlynn Williams, a Pan American flight attendant, was a member of the crew commemorating the anniversary of the airline's 100,000th transatlantic flight. Williams shared a very important anniversary with Pan Am. She was born on June 28, 1939, the day that Pan American inaugurated transatlantic passenger service. Kenlynn Williams had been a flight attendant with Pan Am since August 7, 1961. (Private Collection.)

Pan Am's Miami cargo agents celebrated the first jet cargo flight with this cake. The types of cargo carried on board Pan Am's jet freighters were almost limitless. As Pan Am blazed new trails with passenger service, the company that promised cargo shippers, "We'll work with you!" was the first to operate the 707-321C pure jet freighter and the first airline to operate around-the-world jet freighters. (Florida State Archives.)

Like a beacon to all of New York City, the majestic 56-story Pan Am Building located on New York's prestigious Park Avenue served as the company's corporate headquarters. Designed by Walter Gropius and Pietro Belluschi, the Pan Am Building was the largest corporate office building to be constructed to date. The trademark Pan Am name and its blue world logo crowned the top of the building. (Private Collection.)

Just as Juan Trippe had wanted the Boeing 707 and 747 jets, he also wanted a supersonic transport for Pan Am. Others did not and argued that it could never be economical. Pan Am ordered both the Anglo-French and American versions of supersonic transports (SST). The controversy over the American SST project ended in November 1970 when the U.S. Senate voted against it. In 1971, the project was terminated. (Private Collection.)

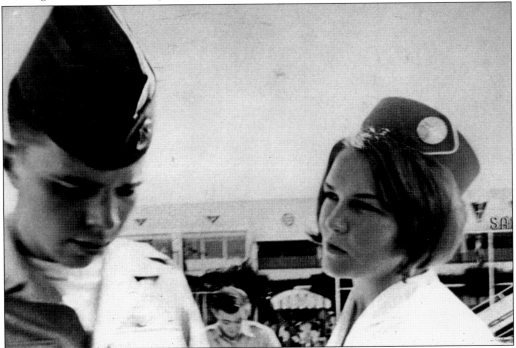

Pan American made a major contribution to America's military airlift requirements as part of the Vietnam War. Millions of pounds of cargo and thousands of troops were transported to Saigon and other ports. War-worn American GIs welcomed the sight of a Pan Am rest-and-recuperation aircraft and the smile of a friendly flight attendant. Each week, Pan Am provided approximately 40 flights between the United States and Vietnam. (Private Collection.)

Juan Trippe and Pan Am shocked the airline industry on April 13, 1966, when an order was placed for 25 wide-body Boeing 747s at a cost of over $500 million. With a cruising speed of 625 miles per hour, the 747 comfortably accommodated 362 passengers. At the company's annual meeting in 1966, Juan Trippe addressed Pan Am's stockholders on the merits of the Boeing 747. He told the audience, "I believe the 747 superjet program will be a winner. The superjet

will be a really competitive asset for Pan Am. For the air shipper, the superjet will offer cheaper cargo service. For the American economy, the program means new jobs for many forward years, in a critical defense industry. For our government, the superjet means national prestige and a contribution of billions of dollars to balance of payments." The 747 almost put Pan Am out of business. (Private Collection.)

Trippe's assessment of the importance of the Boeing 747 was of course correct. However, Pan Am definitely paid the price literally and figuratively for the honor of being the first customer of this giant aircraft. The Boeing 747 may have been the beginning of the end for Pan Am. The aircraft could not have come at a worse time in the company's history. The United States and the rest of the world were mired in a deep recession; demand for air travel had declined

rather than increased, as forecasted. Pan Am's 747s were forced to operate at less than capacity, generating insufficient income to cover the required massive debt service. Pan Am also lost much of its hoped-for competitive advantage when other airlines soon received their own Boeing 747s. (Florida State Archives.)

Pan American's 747s were plagued by major engine problems and numerous minor bugs that required repair and resulted in frequent cancellations or long delays. The first flight to Europe of *Clipper Young America* in January 1970 was cancelled because of engine problems. Seven hours later, 324 passengers took off in a replacement aircraft, *Clipper Constitution*. (Florida State Archives.)

A Pan Am press release in 1970 described the Boeing 747 as "a $23 million airborne penthouse with four salons in different color schemes, six galleys with one for buffets, a dozen restrooms, and a circular stairway rising to a cocktail lounge in the sky." From the aircraft tug to the silver, glasses, and linens, everything on this new generation of aircraft was designed to offer the public the optimum in service. (Private Collection.)

The 747 offered a passenger amenity found on no other aircraft—a first-class lounge. A spiral staircase led to the roomy lounge on the second level of the airplane. The interior of the lounge was outfitted with a semi-circular sofa, padded card tables, swivel chairs, and a bar. Tall enough to stand up in, the lounge accommodated 16 passengers. (Private Collection.)

Pan Am's 747 cabin was 186 feet long and 20 feet wide. There were three economy sections and one first-class area. In near opulence, the first-class cabin accommodated 58 passengers in plush upholstered swivel seats. While Pan Am was introducing the 747, the company's Pacific routes were coming under siege. America's domestic airlines such as Braniff, Northwest, Western, TWA, American, and Continental began to be awarded Pacific routes. (Private Collection.)

Six galleys onboard Pan Am's 747s were capable of providing meal service to 362 passengers. Snap-in-and-out galleys were prepacked with food and a large assortment of beverages. The time needed to serve meals was reduced by 30 percent as flight attendants used rolling carts instead of carrying meals one at a time. Double galleys such as this allowed walk-through capability and smorgasbord buffets. (Private Collection.)

In 1965, Pan Am's flight attendants' uniforms reflected the fashion style of the period. Over the years, the role of a flight attendant gradually evolved into little more than that of an in-flight hostess. On board Pan Am flights, passengers were able to purchase cocktails, liquors, and cigarettes. For diversions on long flights, attendants offered playing cards, stationery, magazines, games, newspapers, and postcards. (Private Collection.)

Pan American first hired female cabin attendants for its flights from Miami to Latin America in 1943. By 1946, the airline employed women flight attendants on transatlantic and transpacific service. As the new decade of the 1970s dawned, Pan Am stewardesses proudly pose for a publicity photograph. Flight attendants and other Pan Am employees were about to see the structure of their company change forever. The company's only president to date, patriarch Juan Trippe, retired in 1968, plunging the airline into decades of instability and turmoil. At the same time, Pan Am's fleet of aircraft was about to change. In 1971, Pan Am placed the first of its wide-body 747s into service. As never before, the airline's safety seemed constantly in question. Along with major 747 delivery problems, Pan Am underwent a spate of crashes. Airplanes seemed to fall from the sky, and a Pan Am 747 was blown up by terrorists. It was not a good time to be a Pan Am flight attendant. (Private Collection.)

A group of female flight attendants pose inside a 747 engine nacelle for a publicity photograph. Always designed to represent the height of current fashions, the distinctive uniforms of Pan Am stewardesses included skirts, blouses, jackets, hats, high-heeled shoes, and matching purses. Age, height, and weight limits were mandated; physical attractiveness was an unofficial requirement of the job. Images of smiling attendants gave the impression that all was well with the airline. Such was not the case, however. Pan Am in the early 1970s had experienced several crashes. It seemed an epidemic as the airline lost 11 Boeing 707s, a 727, and had several minor ground accidents with the 747. Many of the accidents were attributed to pilot error. (Florida State Archives.)

A Pan Am recruiting brochure in 1970 advised young women to "Get into this world as a Pan Am stewardess." Requirements at the time of hire included a minimum age of 20 and unmarried status. After three and a half weeks of ground training and ten days of in-flight and base training, the brochure promised that "a girl in a Pan Am uniform leads an exciting life" in a career that would be stimulating and "free from monotony and far more than just a job." (Private Collection.)

Pan American, in 1929, became the first airline to employ cabin attendants and serve in-flight meals. By 1977, the airline employed over 4,000 flight attendants, 600 of whom were male. With the ability to speak 38 languages, attendants came from 45 countries. In the 1930s and 1940s, the meals had been cold cuts and sandwiches. Meal service now included special menus, with a choice of diabetic, kosher, salt-free, vegetarian, and Hindu selections. (Private Collection.)

Specially designed cargo and baggage containers that were capable of carrying up to 40,000 pounds of freight were used on Pan Am's 747s. Thirty containers, sixteen for baggage and fourteen for freight, were supposed to be able to be unloaded in only eight minutes. Pan Am promised that the "Last bag should reach the claim area 15 minutes after the plane is at the gate." (Private Collection.)

Pan American had several catchy slogans that were used in their advertising. There was no slogan for the turmoil in the boardroom, however. At the annual meeting in 1968, Juan Trippe announced the unthinkable; he was going to retire. Harold Gray, a long-term "Pan Amer" with much experience, became chairman and chief executive officer. Najeeb Halaby was named president. On May 7, as Trippe stepped down, Gray inherited Pan Am and its problems. (Private Collection.)

Pan American's 747SP model was a smaller version of the full-sized Boeing 747. The special performance aircraft, 47 feet shorter than the original 747, boasted less weight and greater fuel efficiency due to the four Pratt and Whitney JT9D-7 engines. With the 747SP, Pan Am could offer nonstop air service between New York and Tokyo. A Pan Am 747SP set a commercial airline record for flying around the world in only 46 hours. (Private Collection.)

Juan Trippe wanted Pan Am to be all things to all people where transportation was concerned. Trippe viewed as competition the fact that many large corporations frequently flew their executives on private aircraft. His solution to the problem was to form a Business Jets Division in 1963. In concert with the French company Dassault, Pan Am designed and marketed the eight-passenger Falcon jet. (Private Collection.)

Pan Am's Kennedy Airport terminal handled thousands of passengers each day. With the introduction of the wide-bodied Boeing 747s, Pan Am embarked on a program of refurbishment at the Worldport costing in excess of $100 million. To provide optimal passenger service, the Worldport boasted 21 gate positions, a Clipper Club, ticket counters, shops, and restaurants. (Private Collection.)

A Pan Am technician at the company's Guided Missiles Range Division witnessed the launch of *Gemini V* at Cape Kennedy. In the early 1950s, the government requested proposals to build and manage a string of tracking stations for the United States Air Force's guided missile program. Pan Am was awarded the project. Eventually renamed Aerospace Services Division, the highly profitable division employed several thousand people. (Private Collection.)

Pan Am FT
WorldPass

Name										

WorldPass Number								Flight Number

Month / Day	Fare Paid	From PA Departure City	To PA Destination City
	F C Y		

☐ Please send me more WorldPass coupons.

Intended as a marketing tool to help provide the best possible service to Pan Am's frequent fliers, Pan Am's frequent traveler program was implemented in 1974. It was estimated that while these passengers accounted for only five percent of Pan Am's volume, they were responsible for 33 percent of the airline's passenger revenues. (Private Collection.)

Pan Am Express, a commuter airline, used the 42-seat ATR42 to service its short-haul routes throughout the Northeastern United States. The ATR42, a twin-engine turbo-prop manufactured by a European consortium, was ideal for flights of less than 200 miles. (Private Collection.)

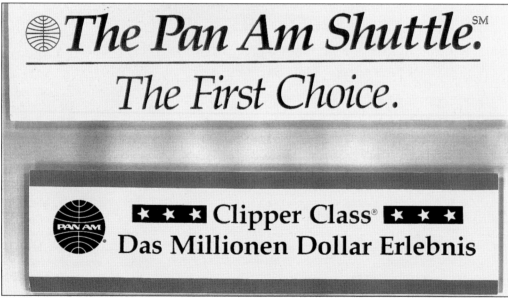

Pan Am's

AIR BRIDGE

14 Flights A Day
Each Way Between
Orlando And
Miami

Using Boeing 727 aircraft, Pan Am's Air Bridge operated a large number of flights from Tampa to Miami and Orlando to Miami. In 1986, Pan Am inaugurated its Northeast Shuttle between Boston, New York, and Washington. Intended as competition for the venerable Eastern Shuttle, the operation served little purpose since it failed to feed passengers to Pan Am's international operations. On September 1, 1991, Delta Airlines acquired the Northeast Shuttle from Pan Am. (Private Collection.)

The Pan Am Shuttle.ᴿ

The First Choice.

★ ★ ★ Clipper Class® ★ ★ ★
Das Millionen Dollar Erlebnis

As Pan American neared the end of its 60th year of service, things were not going well. Campaigns from the marketing department were not reversing the downward spiral. C. Edward Acker was on his way out as chairman. Pan Am and its unions courted several corporations and prospective saviors such as Sir James Goldsmith, Kirk Kerkorian, and Jay A. Pritzker. They all fell through; Thomas Plaskett replaced Acker as chairman. (Private Collection.)

Seven

DEATH OF AN AIRLINE

During the years between 1969 and 1975, Pan Am lost $364 million. Profitability returned in 1976 and 1977, and the company made almost $150 million. As Pan American prepared to enter the 1980s, it was clear that there was trouble ahead. Pan Am's share of the overseas market was drastically shrinking. Chairman William Seawell believed that Pan Am desperately needed a domestic route system. His strategy was to begin buying the stock of the largely domestic Miami-based National Airlines. There was, however, a major problem. Francisco A. Lorenzo, owner of Texas International, also wanted National. On July 9, 1978, Lorenzo informed the Civil Aeronautics Board that he had purchased 9 percent of National's stock. Soon, the war between Pan Am and Lorenzo was on. Each company bought the stock in large blocks. By mid-1978, Pan American and Texas International each owned approximately 25 percent of National's stock. Predictably, the price of the stock continued to escalate. (Private Collection.)

Interim Pan Am/National logo

National's Sungod and Pan Am's globe symbolized the merging of the two airlines. It was not yet to be. Eastern Air Lines began buying National stock. Pan Am offered $50 per share and Lorenzo agreed. Bud Maytag, National's president, and Francisco Lorenzo, Texas International's president, made piles of money on the deal. The $374 million cost of the purchase of National had been too high, however. Pan Am was the big loser. (Private Collection.)

SYVERSON

On January 7, 1980, National Airlines merged with Pan American. In a letter to employees, Seawell wrote, ". . . the end result can be a stronger company and a brighter future for us all." With National's 8,350 employees, there was a great deal of overlap in union and non-union jobs. Merger costs escalated when National employees received pay raises. Financially and operationally, the merger was a disaster. (Private Collection.)

122

Pan Am's Winter and Spring 1980 timetable promised an airline that combined the strength of both carriers. Senior management talked about synergies to be achieved and promised "better customer service to the public." The synergies never materialized, nor did the "better customer service." Long delays became almost routine. (Private Collection.)

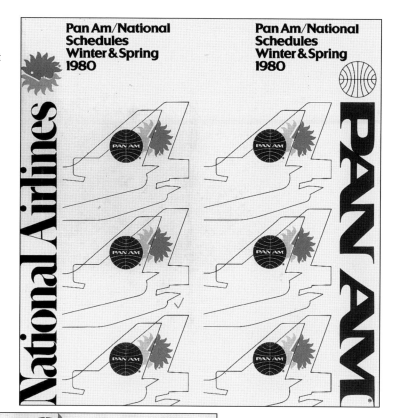

A Special Message to Pan Am and National Passengers

As you may have read, the Pan Am/National Airlines merger has been approved. And now the big job of actually integrating the two air systems begins. So, for the next few months you'll find us working as quickly as we can to dovetail schedules, repaint aircraft, change signs and uniforms. All to make one bigger and better airline. Pan Am.

Airport check-in

In the meantime, both Pan Am and National Airlines will continue to use their separate terminals, check-in counters and gates.

To avoid confusion during the changeover period, Pan Am and National will also continue to use their existing flight schedules and flight numbers.

Reservations & Information

Until the integration of both systems is complete, please continue to call National Airlines reservations offices for reservations or information on National Airlines flights.

For reservations or information on Pan Am flights, please continue to call Pan Am reservations offices.

PAN AM GOES NATIONAL.

"A Special Message to Pan Am and National Passengers" should have advised passengers to be prepared for long delays, lost luggage, and extremely unhappy employees. Rank and file employees of both companies were strongly opposed to the merger. Pan Am's large cash reserves were quickly depleted. The company lost $248 million in 1980. By 1981, Pan Am was losing nearly a million dollars a day! (Private Collection.)

Only 53 years old, William T. Seawell seemed the perfect man to revitalize Pan American. The retired U.S. Air Force brigadier general was a West Point graduate and a product of Harvard Law School. The decorated World War II bomber pilot had also served as commandant of the Air Force Academy. Hired as president of Pan Am on December 1, 1971, Seawell had also gained aviation experience at American Airlines and Rolls-Royce Aero Engines. (Private Collection.)

Following Juan Trippe's retirement from Pan Am in 1968, Harold Gray was named as chairman and Najeeb Halaby as president. A year later, Halaby became chairman; by 1972, he had resigned from Pan Am. In a letter to the New York Times, Halaby blamed many of his problems on Trippe's interference, stating, "He has from time to time intervened in the affairs of the company—particularly in the first five years of his retirement." (Private Collection.)

124

To reduce the huge losses Pan Am was incurring, the company began selling off its assets. The first to go was the Pan Am Building in the heart of Manhattan. The Pan Am Building—that glorious symbol of Pan Am's conquest of the world—was sold to the Metropolitan Life Insurance Company in 1981 for $400 million. (Private Collection.)

The Intercontinental Hotel in Manila, the Philippine Islands, was part of Pan Am's very profitable hotel chain. In the early 1980s, Pan Am was made up of three subsidiaries—Pan American World Airways, Pan Am World Services, and Intercontinental Hotels. On August 19, 1981, the *Wall Street Journal* announced the sale of the Intercontinental Hotels Corporation to Grand Metropolitan for $500 million. (Private Collection.)

As symbolized by this logo, Juan Trippe's philosophy had been growth. During the 1980s, just the opposite was happening. The empire was being dismantled. The chairman's office was like a game of musical chairs. C. Edward Acker, a veteran of Braniff and Air Florida, replaced William Seawell. Acker started Pan Am's rebirth with new international destinations. Soon he would close them as Pan Am lost $485.3 million in 1982. (Private Collection.)

PACIFIC SERVICE

PAA

Printed in U.S.A.

PAN AMERICAN AIRWAYS SYSTEM

At first, Pan Am's employees welcomed Acker, but the honeymoon quickly soured. Labor relations were at an all time nadir. On February 28, 1985, five labor unions went on strike against Pan Am for over a week. The fire sale Seawell had started continued under Acker's administration. In 1985, Pan Am's Pacific Division was sold to United Airlines for $750 million. In addition to the highly profitable Pacific routes, United also received 18 airplanes and 2,700 Pan Am employees. (Private Collection.)

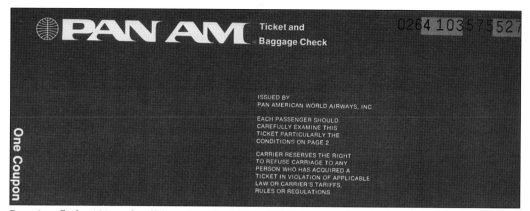

Pan Am flight 103 took off from London's Heathrow Airport shortly after 6 p.m. on December 21, 1988. The captain headed toward New York. By 7 p.m., Pan Am 103 was at an altitude of 31,000 feet; Lockerbie, Scotland, was 5 miles below. Three minutes later, a bomb destroyed the airplane. Two hundred and fifty-nine passengers and crew died. Another 11 people on the ground lost their lives. The effects of Pan Am 103 were predictable and immediate. The airline's passenger traffic plummeted. For the company, it was almost over. (Private Collection.)

On January 20, 1988, Thomas Plaskett replaced Acker as chairman and chief executive officer of Pan Am. In an attempt to stem a $2 million-a-day loss, Plaskett sold additional routes and airplanes to United Airlines for $400 million in 1990. Pan Am gave up the right to fly to London from cities on America's east and west coasts. Pan Am also lost the Washington-to-Paris route. The company's internal German service was later sold to Lufthansa for $150 million. (Private Collection.)

America's Going To Europe This Summer On Pan Am.

CLIPPER MAGAZINE

PAN AM

THE
WINDOWS
OF
NEW YORK

ST. JEAN-CAP-FERRA

Pan Am's *Clipper* magazine provided information and entertainment for the company's dwindling passengers. With few remaining assets, drastically depleted cash reserves, and huge losses, Pan Am filed for Chapter 11 bankruptcy in January 1991. Seven months later, Delta Airlines bought Pan Am's northeastern shuttle operation and the remaining North Atlantic routes. On December 4, 1991, Pan Am, once the world's most experienced airline and now only a shell of its former self, shut down. (Private Collection.)

Juan T. Trippe, founder and long time chairman of Pan American World Airways, once stated, "In the field of air transport, the true objective is to bring to the life of the average man those things which once were the privilege of only the fortunate few." For 64 years, Juan Trippe's Pan Am had done just that. It brought America to the world. (Private Collection.)

PAN AM ®